Painting Borders
FOR YOUR HOME
with Donna Dewberry

NORTH LIGHT BOOKS
CINCINNATI, OHIO
www.artistsnetwork.com

Other fine North Light Books are available from your local bookstore or art supply store, or direct from the publisher.

09 08 07 06 05   5 4 3 2 1

Library of Congress Cataloging-in-Publication Data

Dewberry, Donna S.
    Painting borders for your home with Donna Dewberry
       p. cm.
    Includes index.
    ISBN 1-58180-600-0 (pbk. : alk. paper) -- ISBN 1-58180-599-3 (hc. : alk. paper)
    1. Painting--Technique. 2. Decoration and ornament. 3. Borders, Ornamental (Decorative arts) I. Title

TT385.D4842397 2005
747'.3--dc22
                            2004057570

METRIC CONVERSION CHART		
TO CONVERT	TO	MULTIPLY BY
Inches	Centimeters	2.54
Centimeters	Inches	0.4
Feet	Centimeters	30.5
Centimeters	Feet	0.03
Yards	Meters	0.9
Meters	Yards	1.1
Sq. Inches	Sq. Centimeters	6.45
Sq. Centimeters	Sq. Inches	0.16
Sq. Feet	Sq. Meters	0.09
Sq. Meters	Sq. Feet	10.8
Sq. Yards	Sq. Meters	0.8
Sq. Meters	Sq. Yards	1.2
Pounds	Kilograms	0.45
Kilograms	Pounds	2.2
Ounces	Grams	28.3
Grams	Ounces	0.035

EDITOR: Christina D. Read
PRODUCTION COORDINATOR: Kristen D. Heller
DESIGNER: Clare Finney
LAYOUT ARTIST: Kathy Gardner
PHOTOGRAPHERS: Christine Polomsky, Veronica Ankarörn, Andrea Vankirk

F+W PUBLICATIONS, INC.

A Note From Donna

I have always found it amazing what a little bit of color or design can do to a plain wall. Borders can be inexpensive and fun. They add that certain little touch that your room might be missing. In this book, you will learn how to create and paint your own borders. We will show you a variety of borders for all the rooms in your house. Here is the fun you have been waiting for, so get started on those borders!

ABOUT THE AUTHOR

Donna Dewberry, a native Floridian, has been involved with arts and crafts all of her married life—over thirty years. After many evenings of painting at her dining room table, she developed a technique for stress-free painting that became the basis for the One Stroke™ technique and her series of One Stroke™ painting books.

Donna has kept the vision of the important basic things needed for a happy and successful life—her family, her religion, and her painting. It's true in painting that there are some important basic techniques that every painter needs to know for success. Once you learn and practice the basics of the One Stroke™ technique, you will be able to paint any design in this book. Donna continues to strive to motivate and inspire others and hopes this book will open a door for your future in One Stroke™.

ACKNOWLEDGMENTS

When I think of the hard work that went into creating this book, my heart is full. I am thankful every day for all the wonderful people I am surrounded by. I want to dedicate this book to everyone who contributed in some way. Thank you to the photographers, Christine, Weronica and Andrea and to my editor, Chris. To my son Marcus for his hard work and creativity. To Mike for creating beautiful furniture. To Kerry, Michelle, Maribel, Althea and Terri for their long hours and dedication. To my son Joel and daughter-in-law Laurie for welcoming us into their home, even with Laurie being "very pregnant." To my grandchildren Brendan and Brooke for their excitement and enthusiasm. I love you all and could not have done this without you.

contents

3   A Note From Donna

6   Materials and Techniques

THE PROJECTS

22   Vines & Berries

32   Fantasy Fruit

46   Words to Live By

54   Scrolls

58   Green Meadow

66   Tone-on-Tone

70   Dreamy Lettering

74   Whimsical Daisy

80   Crowning Glory

84   Palm Fronds

88   Grapevines

98   Clothesline

104   Animal Parade

116   Magic Beanstalk

126   Resources

127   Index

materials & techniques

Paint

FOLKART PAINTS

Plaid FolkArt acrylic colors are high-quality bottled acrylic paints. Their rich and creamy formulation and long open time make them perfect for decorative painting. They are offered in a wide range of wonderful premixed colors and in gleaming metallic shades.

FOLKART ARTISTS' PIGMENTS

These deep, true colors blend easily and maintain vibrancy when mixed. Artists' Pigments have a higher pigment concentration than regular FolkArt paints. Therefore, they're better for creating a more intense coverage. Because Artists' Pigments are acrylic paints, they're easy to clean up.

FOLKART METALLIC PAINTS

Here are paints to add beautiful metallic shine to your projects. These paints are highly pigmented. They are also water-based acrylics and can be cleaned up with soap and water.

FOLKART FLOATING MEDIUM

Floating medium allows the paint to stay wetter, which helps with your brush strokes. When painting the One Stroke techniques, please do not follow the instructions on the bottle. This will make your strokes very muddy looking. Instead, load your brush as instructed in the Techniques Chapter, then dip the tip of the bristles straight down into the puddle of floating medium. Stroke two or three times on your palette. Now you are ready to paint.

Brushes

FLAT BRUSHES

Painting the One Stroke technique requires the use of flat brushes. The Donna Dewberry One Stroke Brushes are designed with longer bristles and less thickness in the brush body to allow for a much sharper chisel edge. A sharp chisel edge is essential to the success of the One Stroke technique, since most strokes begin and end on the chisel edge.

ANGULAR BRUSHES

Angular brushes can make it easier to paint such things as rose petals and vines. The One Stroke angular brushes come in ⅜-inch (10mm), ⅝-inch (16mm) and ¾-inch (19mm) sizes.

SCRUFFY BRUSHES

The scruffy brush that I have created is ready to be used straight from the package. All you have to do is "fluff the scruff." Remove the brush from the package and form the natural hair bristles into an oval shape by gently pulling on them. Then twist the bristles in your palm until you have an oval shape. Now you are ready to pounce into the paint and begin. When fluffed, the scruffy brush is used for painting moss, wisteria, lilacs, some hair and fur, faux painting and shading textures. Do not use this brush with water. To clean the scruffy brush, pounce the bristles into the brush basin. Do not rake them or you will break the natural hair bristles.

LINER BRUSHES

There are two sizes of liner brushes. The no. 1 script liner (sometimes referred to as the mini) is usually used for small detail work when more control is needed. The no. 2 script liner is used when less control is needed.

The liner brush is used with paint of an "inky" consistency. To create this consistency, pour a small amount of paint onto your palette. Dip the liner brush into water, then touch the water to your palette, next to the paint. Do this three or four times. Roll your brush where the water and paint meet to mix them until you have an inky consistency. Don't mix all of the paint with the water or your mixture will be too thick. Roll the brush out of the inky paint to prevent it from dripping. See page 12 for instructions on how to load the liner brush. Clean these brushes the same way as the scruffy brushes. Once again, be gentle but clean them thoroughly.

Supplies

PALETTE & BRUSH CADDY

The FolkArt One Stroke Palette and Brush Caddy that I use are durable and handy. The palette has numerous paint

---

SUPPLIES (SHOWN AT RIGHT)
1. One Stroke brushes 2. FolkArt Artists' Pigments 3. FolkArt Brush Caddy
4. FolkArt One Stroke Paint Palette 5. sponge painter 6. graphite paper
7. FolkArt Floating Medium (left) and FolkArt Metallic Paints (right) 8. tracing
paper 9. FolkArt Acrylic Paints 10. sponge painters 11. FolkArt Acrylic Lacquers

wells, is designed for left- or right-handed use, and holds a 9-inch (23cm) disposable foam plate.

SPONGE PAINTER

These special sponge painters soften edges. They allow you to paint both large, open surfaces and tight spaces, as well as corners.

FOLKART ACRYLIC LACQUERS

These fast-drying spray-on lacquers are formulated to use indoors and out. They leave a smooth, clear, even finish and diminish naturally occurring imperfections in wood. They are for use on wood and metal surfaces

TRANSFERRING THE PATTERN

Patterns for all the projects in this book are provided for you. The easiest way to transfer a pattern to your chosen surface is to first enlarge the pattern to the percentage given (any photocopy center can do this for you). Then place a piece of tracing paper over the enlarged pattern. Trace the pattern with a pen.

Now position the tracing paper on your surface and tape it down in a few places with low-tack tape. Slide some graphite paper in between the tracing paper and the surface, making sure the graphite side is toward the surface.

Using a stylus or pencil, trace only the outer edges of the design's major elements, not all the details. Check your work by lifting up a corner every once in a while to make sure you haven't missed a line. Remove the graphite and the tracing paper, and you're ready to paint!

PARTS OF THE BRUSH

CHISEL
This is the edge of the flat or the angle brush bristles.

HEEL
This is the term for the short bristles of the angle brush.

TOE
This is the term for the long bristles of the angle brush.

TIME-SAVING TIP
To save time when starting a project, properly load every brush you will be using ahead of time. Dip the tip of each handle into the main color on the loaded brush, then place all the brushes into the filled water basin/brush caddy. When you are ready to paint, take your brush out and lay it on a fresh paper towel to drain the excess water. Brush back and forth across the palette a few times until you are ready to go.

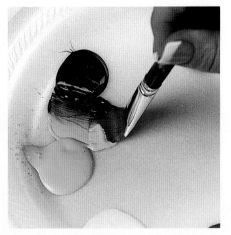

LOADING THE BRUSH

1 Dip the corner.

2 Dip the other corner into the second color.

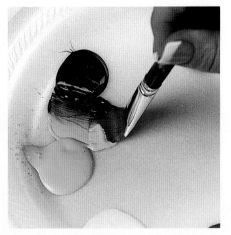

3 Stroke one way.

4 Stroke the other way. Be sure not to make the loading area longer than 2 inches (5cm). That way, the paint works into the brush.

5 Dip the brush again, into both colors, and work the paint in again.

MULTI-LOADING

1 Double load first.

3 Stroke back and forth a couple of times to work the paint into the brush. Then start painting.

2 Dip the darker corner into the darker color and the lighter corner into the lighter color.

ADDING FLOATING MEDIUM

1 Take your loaded brush and dip straight into your floating medium.

2 Work it in twice and then paint.

LOADING THE SCRUFFY & POUNCING

1 Fluff the scruffy brush first. If it is brand new, dip it in water to remove the sizing.

2 Pounce half the brush into the paint, pouncing straight up and down.

3 Turn the brush around and pounce the other half into the second color. Never dip the corners into the paint. Pounce every time.

4 Pounce and move the brush around.

5 See art above. The left side is done correctly.

6 Tip just the edge of the brush.

LOADING THE ANGLE BRUSH

1 The color that should be out of the way is placed on the heel of the brush. Dip the toe of the brush into the second color.

2 Stroke back and forth to work in the color.

LOADING THE SCRIPT LINER

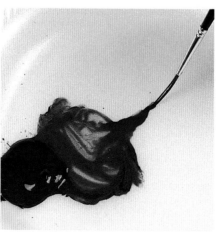

Dip the no. 2 script liner completely in water. Using a circular motion next to a puddle of paint, allow the tips of the bristles to touch the paint, mixing the water with the paint to make an inky consistency. Add more water as necessary. Repeat three times.

MAKING CURLICUES

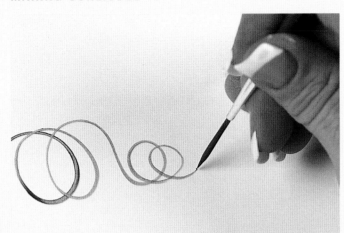

Take an ink pen and make Ms across the page to practice. Move your arm in the direction in which you will be painting. Take the brush and practice the following movement with water: make three loops, reverse direction and do tight curls in the reverse way. Hold the brush in the same way as you would hold a pencil, resting the brush on the first knuckle of your supporting finger. Load with paint and paint curlicues.

LOADING THE FILBERT BRUSH

1 Load one color on a flat side of the brush. Load the light color first.

2 Turn the brush over and load the dark color.

PAINTING VINES WITH AN ANGLE BRUSH

1 It is sometimes easier to use an angle brush to paint a vine rather than a flat. If you want a thin vine, use the chisel and pull with the toe.

2 Start on one side and cross over to the other side. Go along the vine and add additional branches. Continue to do this to make the vine as full as you choose.

. . . AND A FLAT BRUSH

Touch on the chisel, tilt the yellow side up and then drag the green behind.

SHELL

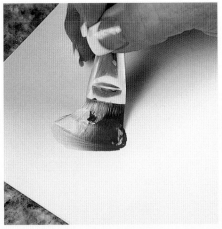

1 Stroke back and forth, then move your brush as if you were scrubbing the surface. Scrub and watch your width as you are pulling the stroke.

2 To end the stroke, slide down.

HEART-SHAPED LEAF WITH WIGGLES

1 Tap your brush to paint your "V".

2 Lay the bristles down and paint a C-stroke, then lift. Repeat three more times.

3 Lay bristles down, wiggle back and forth, pivoting on the yellow side and turning the green to form a shell.

4 Stand your brush up and slide it to the top. Watch the outside edge to create the shape. Repeat the same step on the outside edge, including the 1–2–3 starter stroke.

5 Using the chisel edge of the brush, lead with the light color then pull the stem halfway into the leaf.

MULTI-STROKE LEAF

1 Paint big teardrops. The last stroke is like a one-stroke leaf on the end.

2 Push to get the width of the leaf and slide the yellow side of the brush to the tip.

3 Paint the other side of the leaf like one large teardrop. Using the chisel edge of the brush, lead with the light color, then pull the stem halfway into the leaf.

PAINTING A ONE-STROKE LEAF

1 Push down.

2 Turn.

3 Slide as you lift to a point.

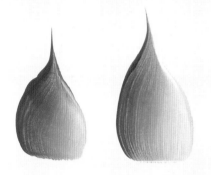

SKINNY LEAVES

1 Touch on the chisel and slide as if you were making a branch.

2 As you slide, lean forward and use pressure to make the leaf the width you desire. Pull back to the chisel as you slide.

FIVE-PETAL FLOWERS

1 Tap on the "V" first. Paint the curved stroke to start and finish between the Vs. Make sure your brush handle stays straight up.

2 Paint these strokes all the way around. Paint at least five petals.

3 To form a cluster, layer your groups of petals. For a trailing petal, angle your brush down, chisel, lean and pull. Dot the center.

C-STROKE

1 Tap in your lines to give direction. Paint a C-shaped stroke. Watch the top edge.

COMMA STROKE

1 Get on the chisel with a lot of paint.

2 Touch at an angle, use pressure and pull to the chisel.

20

SPONGING A SHAPE

Pull the white paint from the plate and side load the other color on the edge. Apply pressure on the edge to create the shape of your object. Rub in a circular motion.

TRANSFERRING LETTERING

1 Place your pattern over graphite paper and your surface, making sure the graphite side is towards the surface. Use a pen or pencil to trace.

vine & berries

I wanted my guests to leave my home with a smile, remembering the visit and my love for nature. The vines remind me that our lives are intertwined with our family and friends. I hope when guests walk through our door they feel that they are part of our lives.

You may want to add a few more insects or more birds, similar to the ones I painted, for added interest.

PAINT: (A)=FOLKART ACRYLIC; (AP)=FOLKART ARTISTS' PIGMENTS

Alizarin Crimson (AP)

Burnt Carmine (AP)

Burnt Sienna (AP)

Burnt Umber (AP)

Linen (A)

Thicket (A)

Wicker White (A)

Yellow Ochre (AP)

SURFACE
• wall

BRUSHES
• ¾-inch (19mm) flat
• 1-inch (25mm) flat
• no. 12 flat
• no. 16 flat
• no. 1 script liner
• no. 2 script liner

ADDITIONAL SUPPLIES
• floating medium

PAINT COLORS FOR COORDINATING BORDER

Burnt Carmine (AP)

Burnt Umber (AP)

Engine Red (A)

Linen (A)

Thicket (A)

Wicker White (A)

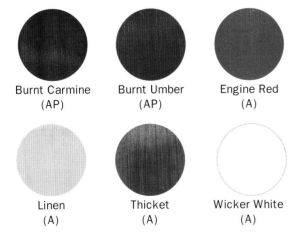
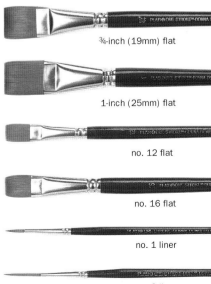

¾-inch (19mm) flat

1-inch (25mm) flat

no. 12 flat

no. 16 flat

no. 1 liner

no. 2 liner

This pattern may be hand-traced or photo-copied for personal use only. Enlarge at 182% to bring up to full size.

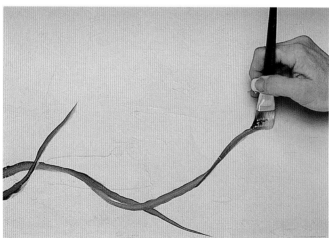

1 **PAINTING THE VINE** Add floating medium as needed throughout this project to keep the paint smooth and the colors soft. Double load a 1-inch (25mm) flat with Burnt Umber and Linen using the chisel edge and leading with Linen. Paint the vines. Occasionally add some Wicker White to the Linen side.

2 Add some small, trailing vines off of the main vine.

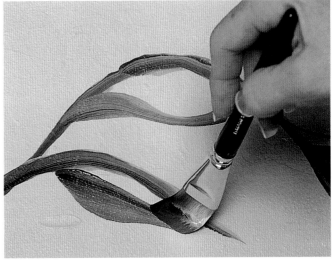

3 **PAINT THE LEAVES** Using the same brush and same colors, add a touch of Thicket to the Burnt Umber side. Using the flat side of the brush, paint the long one-stroke leaves.

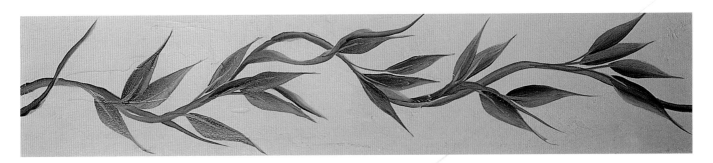

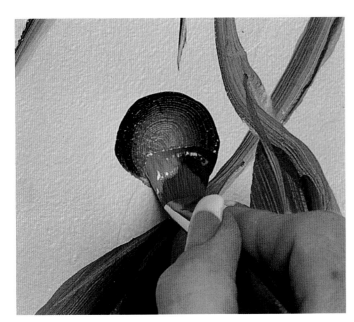

4 **PAINT THE PODS** Double load a no. 16 flat with Yellow Ochre, Alizarin Crimson, then side load a touch of Burnt Carmine on the Alizarin Crimson side. Paint the pods.

5 Using the same brush and colors, touch on the chisel edge, lean towards the pod and then pull, leading with the red color towards the pod.

6 Using the no. 2 script liner and Alizarin Crimson, paint a C-stroke where the chisel-edge strokes meet.

7 Double load the no. 16 flat with Linen and Burnt Umber; add a stem to the pods.

8 **PAINT THE BERRIES** Load the no. 12 flat with Alizarin Crimson and then side load a touch of Burnt Carmine. Paint small berries.

9 Load a no. 2 script liner with inky Burnt Umber and then stroke through the puddle of Linen. Touch to highlight the berries and pull stems to the branches.

10 **ADD SHADING & CURLICUES** Load a no. 16 flat with floating medium and then side load a touch of Burnt Umber to add shading underneath the leaves and vines. Use the no. 1 script liner with Thicket to paint curlicues.

11 **PAINT THE HEAD & BACK OF THE BIRD** Double load a no. 12 flat with Linen and Burnt Umber and some floating medium. Keep the Burnt Umber to the top and base in the top of the head and back of the bird.

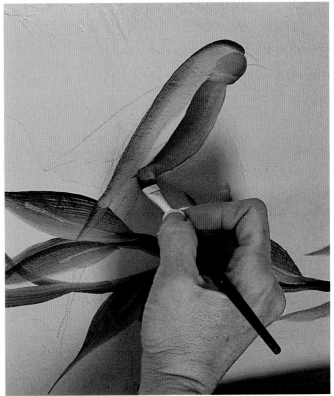

12 **PAINT THE CHEEK & BODY** With the same brush, pick up Yellow Ochre and Burnt Sienna, using the flat side of the brush and keeping the Burnt Sienna to the outside edge, to paint the bird's cheek. Flip the brush and have the Yellow Ochre to the outside to paint the bottom part of the body.

"The vines remind me that our lives are intertwined with family and friends."

27

13 **PAINT THE SHOULDER** Double load a ¾-inch (19mm) flat with Burnt Sienna, Alizarin Crimson and a touch of Burnt Umber to the Alizarin Crimson side. Paint the shoulder of the wing.

14 **PAINT THE FEATHERS** Use the chisel edge of the same brush to paint the feathers, picking up Yellow Ochre to add contrast.

15 Paint a second layer of feathers.

16 **PAINT THE TAIL FEATHERS** To paint the tail feathers, use the same colors and brush and chisel, starting at the bottom.

USING A COORDINATING BORDER IN ANOTHER LOCATION

Here's an example of a coordinating border painted on a set of doors, to harmonize with the main border found on pages 22 and 30-31.

Use this border to add detailing to walls, doors, furniture or use your imagination to coordinate with the large vine and berry border.

17 **PAINTING THE BEAK** Use a no. 2 script liner with Yellow Ochre and a touch of Burnt Umber to paint the beak.

18 **PAINTING THE EYE, ACCENTING THE BEAK** For the eye, paint a small circle with Burnt Umber using a no. 1 script liner. Dot with Wicker White for highlight. Pick up Burnt Carmine to paint an accent on the beak.

19 **SHADING THE BIRD** Load a no. 16 flat with floating medium and then side load a touch of Burnt Umber to add shading underneath the bird. Keep the Burnt Umber side toward the bird.

20 **FINISHING TOUCHES** Add the final details, such as shading or highlighting, to the border.

fantasy fruit

Using a table that had seen better days was the beginning of this room's transformation. The wear and tear had spilled over to the chairs as well. So we decided to bring it all together and tie the design to the surrounding walls. Use the fruit from your favorite dishes as inspiration for your design.

PAINT: (A)=FOLKART ACRYLIC; (AP)=FOLKART ARTISTS' PIGMENTS

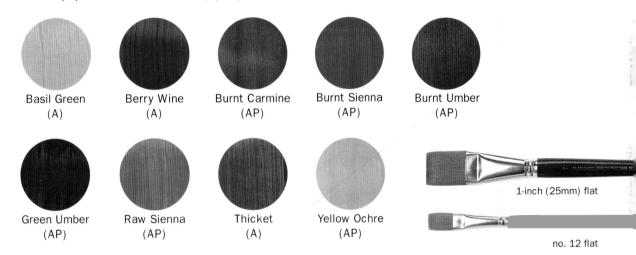

Basil Green
(A)

Berry Wine
(A)

Burnt Carmine
(AP)

Burnt Sienna
(AP)

Burnt Umber
(AP)

Green Umber
(AP)

Raw Sienna
(AP)

Thicket
(A)

Yellow Ochre
(AP)

1-inch (25mm) flat

no. 12 flat

PAINT COLORS FOR COORDINATING BORDER

Berry Wine
(A)

Sunflower
(A)

Thicket
(A)

Yellow Ochre
(AP)

SURFACE
- wall
- table

BRUSHES
- 1-inch (25mm) flat
- no. 12 flat

ADDITIONAL SUPPLIES
- damp white rag
- sponge painter

1 **SPONGE THE BACKGROUND COLOR** Sponge background with Raw Sienna, Burnt Sienna and a touch of Yellow Ochre.

These patterns may be hand-traced or photocopied for personal use only. Enlarge at 200%, then enlarge again at 111% to bring up to full size.

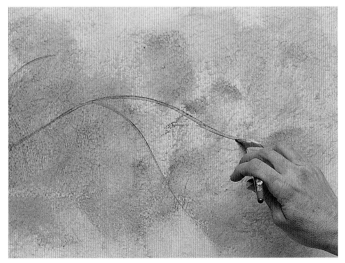

2 **PAINT THE VINE** Double load a 1-inch (25mm) flat with Green Umber and Thicket. Add Basil Green on the Thicket side and occasionally add a touch of Burnt Carmine. Using the chisel edge and leading with the light color, paint the vine.

3 **ADD LEAVES** Using the same brush and colors and the flat side of the brush, add some long, skinny leaves.

4 **ADD LARGE GRAPE LEAVES** Still using the same brush and colors, add some large grape leaves with the Green Umber to the outer edge. Wiggle out and slide in for the largest part of the leaf.

5 Wiggle back out and slide back to the center for the next sections.

6 Push down and wiggle to the tip to finish the leaf.

7 Pull a stem halfway into the leaf using the chisel edge.

8 **PAINT THE STEM AND FERN LEAVES** Using the same brush and colors, paint the stem on the chisel and then dab the fern leaves onto the wall.

9 Work up and down, add more leaves to the fern, using the chisel of the brush.

10 **PAINT THE PALM FRONDS** For the palm fronds, paint the stem and then pull the long, slender leaves from the stem—push, pull, lift, push, pull, lift.

11 **PAINT THE PEAR** Double load the 1-inch (25mm) flat with Yellow Ochre, Burnt Carmine and add a touch of Burnt Umber to the Yellow Ochre side of the brush. Use the flat side of the brush and keep the Burnt Carmine to the outer edge. Paint the first half of the pear.

12 Flip the brush and paint the second half.

13 Fill in the center.

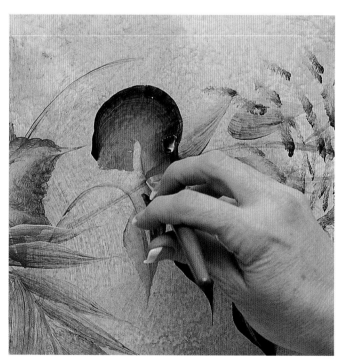

14 **PAINT THE PLUM** Using the same brush and colors, paint a large C-stroke for the plum.

15 Paint a large teardrop, overlapping the first stroke.

16 Add the second plum, overlapping the first plum and following the same directions.

17 **PAINT THE GREEN PEARS** Double load the 1-inch (25mm) flat with Thicket and Basil Green, adding a touch of Yellow Ochre to the Basil Green side. Using the flat side of the brush and keeping the Thicket to the outer edge, paint the green pears with the same procedure as the red pears.

18 **PAINT THE GRAPES** Double load the no. 12 flat with Berry Wine and Burnt Carmine, keeping the Burnt Carmine to the outer edge. Paint a C-stroke. Flip the brush to paint the second half. You're trying to create the "illusion" and not perfection. Trail the grapes down as if they were on a branch.

19 Here is the finished bunch of grapes.

20 **FILL IN EMPTY SPACES** Fill in the empty areas with long, skinny one-stroke leaves, overlapping part of the fruit. Use the same dirty brush used to paint the grapes. Add some Thicket, Yellow Ochre or Burnt Umber. Paint a few large one-stroke leaves, using the 1-inch (25mm) brush and the same variety of colors.

21 **CREATING AN AGED FINISH** Let the paint dry well. Then take a damp, white, terry cloth rag and rub off some of the paint to create an aged finish.

22 **CREATING AN ANTIQUED EFFECT** Take a moistened sponge painter loaded with a touch of Burnt Sienna. Rub lightly over your entire painted area to create an antiqued effect.

USING A COORDINATING BORDER One of the elements of the large border—the pears—was chosen for a coordinating border. This border can be painted on accent linens or other accessories in this or an adjoining room.

TABLE CORNER

These patterns may be hand-traced or photocopied for personal use only. Enlarge at 200%, then enlarge again at 125% to bring up to full size.

BACK OF CHAIR

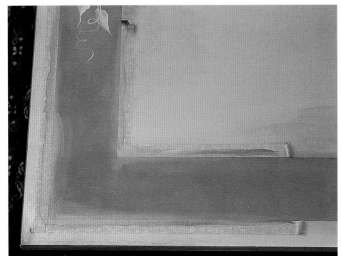

1 PAINTING THE BORDER Tape off the size you want for the border and basecoat with Green Umber.

2 PAINTING VINES & LEAVES Paint the vines and the leaves (see instructions on p. 35).

3 **PAINTING THE PEARS** Paint the gold pear using Yellow Ochre and a touch of Berry Wine (see instructions for painting a pear, starting on p. 37).

4 Paint the red pear.

5 **PAINT THE PLUMS** Paint the plums (see instructions on p. 38–39).

6 **PAINT THE GRAPES** Now paint the grapes (see instructions on p. 39).

7 **ADD LEAVES & FERNS** Fill in with more leaves and ferns (see instructions on pgs. 35-37) by using Burnt Carmine and Yellow Ochre to stand out against the green paint on the table.

8 **ADD CURLICUES** Paint some curlicues. Allow to completely dry.

9 **FINISHING TOUCHES** DO NOT RUB PAINT OFF OF THE TABLE. Antique the painted area (see instructions on p. 41). Finish with spray lacquer in your choice of finishes.

FINISHED TABLE TOP

My husband and I designed and built the table and chairs. We chose the words one by one. They reminded us of the kind, patient and caring children we raised. We hope our grandchildren will also believe and understand the gifts that are received from love, hope, charity and more. Aren't these the wishes we all have for a happy family life?

Displaying a message of your thoughts in your home, whether on a table or on a wall, will allow those thoughts to be shared with your family and friends. It is an easy way to show examples of who you are and what you believe in.

PAINT: (A)=FOLKART ACRYLICS; (AP)=FOLKART ARTISTS' PIGMENTS

Alizarin Crimson
(AP)

Basil Green
(A)

Burnt Sienna
(AP)

Burnt Umber
(AP)

Yellow Ochre
(AP)

Engine Red
(A)

Raw Sienna
(AP)

Tapioca
(A)

Thicket
(A)

SURFACE
• wooden table and chairs

BRUSHES
• ³/₄-inch (19mm) flat
• 1-inch (25mm) flat
• no. 2 script liner
• no. 4 round
  (no photo available)

ADDITIONAL SUPPLIES
• sponge painter
• floating medium
• graphite paper
• Plaid FolkArt
  Crackle Medium

PAINT COLORS FOR COORDINATING BORDER

Alizarin Crimson
(AP)

Basil Green
(A)

Burnt Carmine
(AP)

Engine Red
(A)

Thicket
(A)

Yellow Ochre
(AP)

¾-inch (19mm) flat

1-inch (25mm) flat

no. 2 script liner

HOW TO CRACKLE YOUR SURFACE

Before you start painting, crackle the surface. Here are directions on how to crackle: Basecoat with the color of your choice. Let dry. Apply Plaid FolkArt Crackle Medium (either brush or roll on). Let dry–it is dry when it is NOT sticky to the touch (allow about 1-2 hours). Apply the topcoat. (The heavier the coat, the larger the cracks. The thinner the coat, the smaller the cracks. Try not to overlap the strokes. Let dry completely.) Use either a lighter or darker shade, or use the same color for a tone-on-tone look. When the topcoat is dry, seal with a matte or satin spray lacquer. (Using a brush-on sealer could ruin the crackling.) Now you are ready to paint on your surface or antique.

TAKE NOTE: Crackling works best where the humidity is low. If you live in a humid climate, work in air conditioning.

These patterns may be hand-traced or photocopied for personal use only. Enlarge at 200%, then enlarge again at 200% to bring up to full size. Print your lettering using a computer in the font and size desired. There are many web sites available that have a variety of fonts available. This is a script font.

For this scroll and pod pattern only, enlarge at 200% and then enlarge again at 147%.

Family   Sharing

Friendship   Eternity

Nurture   Dreams

1 LETTERING THE SURFACE

Transfer your lettering onto the table using graphite paper. Choose the dark or light graphite paper that works best on the color of your table. Use a no. 4 round brush with thinned Tapioca. Use the tip of the brush to paint all the thin upward strokes. Do not put pressure on upward strokes. This is similar to writing with a pen. As you stroke down you apply pressure to make your strokes thicker; as you stroke up, use less pressure.

2 **THICKER DOWNWARD STROKES** For the thicker downward strokes, apply pressure to spread the bristles. Paint the words. Let dry completely. Use a damp cloth to wash off the remaining graphite.

3 **ADD SHADING TO THE LETTERING** Load a no. 2 script liner with inky Burnt Umber. Add the shading to one side of the letters. Keep all shading on the same side of each letter.

4 **PAINT THE VINE** Double load a 1-inch (25mm) flat with Thicket and Basil Green. Add a touch of Burnt Umber on the Thicket side. Work in a touch of floating medium. Using the chisel edge of the brush and leading with the Basil Green, paint the thin vine.

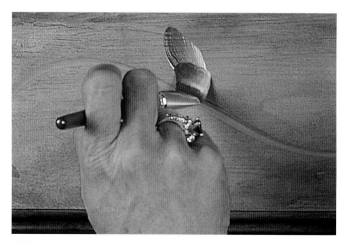

5 **PAINT THE COMMA STROKE** Using the same brush and colors, paint the comma stroke.

6 ADD WIGGLE LEAVES With the same brush, add the wiggle-shaped leaves, using a sliding technique to paint the second half. Occasionally add Yellow Ochre to make lighter leaves and scrolls. Pull a stem into the leaves using the chisel edge.

Displaying a message in your home of your thoughts will allow those thoughts to be shared with your family and friends. It is an easy way to show examples of who you are and what you believe in.

7 PAINT THE PODS Load a ¾-inch (19mm) flat with Yellow Ochre and then side load a touch of Engine Red and Alizarin Crimson.

8 Using the same brush and colors, start on the chisel, leading with Yellow Ochre, and pull towards the pod. Flip the brush to lead with the Engine Red/Alizarin Crimson side to add lighter color strokes.

9 Using the same brush and colors and with Engine Red to the outer edge, touch on the chisel, slide up, stop on the chisel and then slide back down. Paint the outside and then fill in from the top down.

10 **FINISHING STROKES** Add a touch of Burnt Umber and then pull some strokes at the base of each pod.

11 **FINISHING DETAILS** Using the same brush and colors, add a few more comma strokes. Use the script liner and Burnt Umber to add details. Allow to completely dry.

12 **ANTIQUING THE SURFACE** To antique, use the sponge painter alternating with Burnt Sienna, Raw Sienna, Burnt Umber and a small amount of floating medium. Rub over the painted surface, keeping the darker areas to the outside edges.

FINISHED TABLE BORDER & A COORDINATING BORDER The coordinating border (bottom border) picks up the smaller elements of the table border. You can paint this coordinating border on other pieces of furniture in the room, such as a buffet table or on cabinet drawers. Make sure to keep the scale smaller than the table border.

scrolls

The arched entryway into this room inspired the scrolling border I created. The warm Tuscan look reminded me of the many colorful paintings I've seen in my travels. This look never gets dated and goes with many decorating styles. You really can do this project very quickly. And it is versatile enough to work in any décor. It can also be painted on a piece of furniture. Just adjust the size of the strokes or change the colors.

PAINT: (A)=FOLKART ACRYLICS; (AP)=FOLKART ARTISTS' PIGMENTS; (M)=FOLKART METALLICS

| Alizarin Crimson (AP) | Burnt Umber (AP) | Inca Gold (M) | Yellow Ochre (AP) |

SURFACE
- wall

BRUSHES
- ¾-inch (19mm) flat

ADDITIONAL SUPPLIES
- sponge painter
- clean, dampened rag

PAINT COLORS FOR COORDINATING BORDER

| Alizarin Crimson (AP) | Engine Red (A) | Yellow Ochre (AP) |

¾-inch (19mm) flat

A COORDINATING BORDER Although this border is smaller in size and scale, it does have more detail. It would look great above or below a chair rail or painted above a door frame.

55

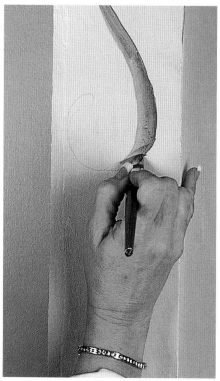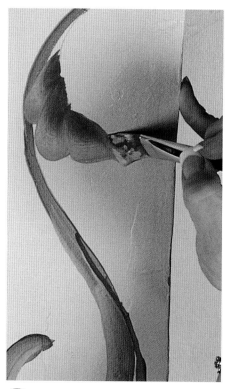

1 **STARTING THE SCROLL** Pencil the design on the wall. Use the ¾-inch (19mm) flat, double loaded with Alizarin Crimson, Burnt Umber, a touch of Yellow Ochre and Inca Gold. Touch on the chisel edge, then lean the bristles down and slide. Lead with the lighter color. Use more pressure for wider areas and less pressure for thinner strokes.

2 **ENDING WITH A COMMA STROKE** As you paint a comma stroke, touch and lean the bristles, then slide in a diagonal direction as you lift to the chisel edge.

3 **ADDING LEAVES TO THE SCROLL** Using the flat side of the brush, lay the bristles down and then wiggle out and in, lifting to the chisel to form the tip.

This pattern may be hand-traced or photo-copied for personal use only. Enlarge at 200%, then enlarge to 185% again to bring up to full size.

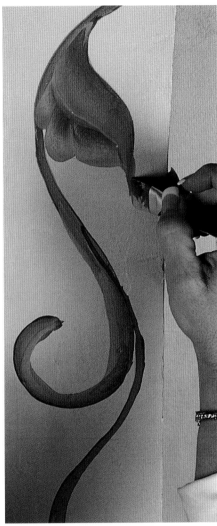

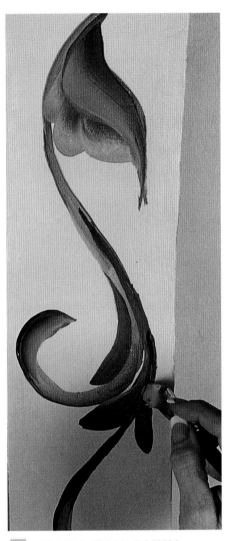

CREATING AN AGED LOOK
6 Using a dampened cloth, rub off some of the paint to give it a worn look.

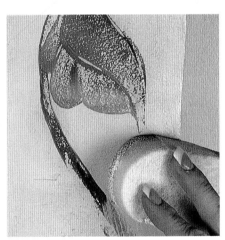

4 To paint the second half of the leaf, lay the flat side of the bristles down and slide as you turn the Yellow Ochre/ Inca Gold to the tip.

5 **ADDING MORE COMMA STROKES** Double load the ¾-inch (19mm) flat with Alizarin Crimson and Yellow Ochre, adding a touch of Burnt Umber to the Alizarin Crimson side and a touch of Inca Gold to the Yellow Ochre side. Add some comma strokes. Let dry for about an hour, until there is no sheen to the paint and it is dry to the touch.

7 Load a dampened sponge painter with a small amount of the wall paint color. Rub lightly over your painting to give it an aged appearance.

green meadow

How do you choose the colors for your bedroom? I start with the bedding set. Then I only paint what I feel will work with the room. Keep it simple and the painting will work even if you change your decor. Iris borders will go with so many other floral patterns, plaids and stripes, solids and more; just keep the colors slightly subdued. Greenery creates a peaceful look and will add a touch of elegance to your bedroom.

PAINT: (A)=FOLKART ACRYLICS; (AP)=FOLKART ARTISTS' PIGMENTS; (M)=FOLKART METALLICS

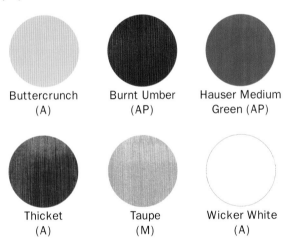

Buttercrunch (A)

Burnt Umber (AP)

Hauser Medium Green (AP)

Thicket (A)

Taupe (M)

Wicker White (A)

SURFACE
• wall

BRUSHES
• 1-inch (25mm) flat
• no. 12 flat
• no. 16 flat
• no. 2 script liner

ADDITIONAL SUPPLIES
• floating medium

PAINT COLORS FOR COORDINATING BORDER

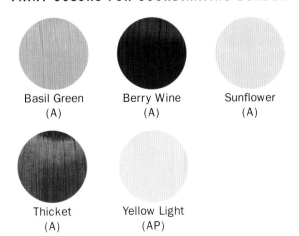

Basil Green (A)

Berry Wine (A)

Sunflower (A)

Thicket (A)

Yellow Light (AP)

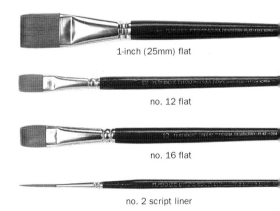

1-inch (25mm) flat

no. 12 flat

no. 16 flat

no. 2 script liner

This pattern may be hand-traced or photocopied for personal use only. Enlarge at 200%, and enlarge again at 156% to bring up to full size.

1 **PAINT THE VINE** Double load a 1-inch (25mm) flat with Buttercrunch and Thicket. Using the chisel edge of the brush and leading with the Buttercrunch, paint the vine. Add additional vines crossing over the main vine.

2 **ADD LEAVES** Using the same brush and colors, add a lot of floating medium to create a slightly transparent color. Using the flat side of the brush, touch, push down, slide and lift to paint the long, thin leaves. Pull a stem halfway into the leaf using the chisel and leading with the lighter color.

3 Load fresh paint on the same brush and then, using the flat side of the brush with Buttercrunch to the outer edge, paint the wiggle leaves.

4 **ADD FERNS** Double load the no. 12 flat with Taupe and floating medium. Paint a series of small one-stroke leaves to simulate ferns.

5 **PAINT ADDITIONAL LEAVES** Using the same dirty brush, load with Thicket and then side load a touch of Burnt Umber; paint additional one-stroke leaves. These darker leaves will add dimension.

6 Using the same dirty brush, add a lot of floating medium and paint some shadowy leaves.

7 **ADD A FLOWERY CLUSTER** Double load the no. 16 flat with Taupe and Wicker White. Using the chisel, touch, lean forward, and pull a long chisel stroke towards a vine to form a light flowery cluster.

8 **PAINT FIVE-PETAL FLOWERS** Using the same brush and colors, and keeping the Taupe to the outer edge, paint five-petal flowers with the flat side of the brush. Make points by lifting to the chisel edge at the outer part of the petals.

9 Double load a no. 12 flat with Hauser Medium Green and Buttercrunch. Touch on the chisel in the center of the flower and then push and pull to form the center.

10 **ADD A TRUMPET FLOWER** Double load a 1-inch (25mm) flat with Wicker White and Buttercrunch, staying mainly on the chisel edge and keeping the Buttercrunch touching a stem. Paint a C-stroke to form the base of the trumpet flower.

11 Using the same brush and colors and keeping Wicker White to the outer edge, paint ripple strokes to form the flower. Try to make at least five petals to form the flower.

12 Still using the same brush and colors and keeping Wicker White to the outer edge, paint the bud. Start at the outer tip of the bud and then touch, lean, and pull. Overlap with a second stroke and then a third and fourth.

13 Use the no. 2 script liner with inky Burnt Umber to pull the stamens outward from the open flower center.

14 Load the no. 2 script liner with Hauser Medium Green and Buttercrunch. Paint a C-stroke at the base of the stamens to add depth.

15 Pick up Burnt Umber on the no. 2 script liner and dot the tips of the stamens.

16 **ADD CURLICUES** Load the no. 2 script liner with inky Thicket. Add a few curlicues to mimic new growth.

**GREEN MEADOW BORDER
& A COORDINATING BORDER**

The coordinating border (the bottom border) is painted in a bolder color combination. If soft, neutral colors aren't to your taste, add some color to your border. Try to pick up hues from your bedding, etc.

tone-on-tone

I wanted to incorporate some painting in my angel room, but I didn't want the painting to overpower the room. It was important to me to keep a classy, soft elegance in this room.

The shimmer from the metallic colors used gave an effect that made me feel that there was a glow of light coming from heaven. I feel that the color white is for purity, and it reminds me that angels are all around us.

PAINT: (A)=FOLKART ACRYLICS; (M)=FOLKART METALLICS

Taupe
(M)

Wicker White
(A)

PAINT COLORS FOR COORDINATING BORDER

Brilliant Blue
(A)

Wicker White
(A)

SURFACE
• wall

BRUSHES
• ¾-inch (19mm) flat
• no. 12 flat

ADDITIONAL SUPPLIES
• floating medium

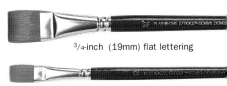

³/₄-inch (19mm) flat lettering

no. 12 flat

The tone-on-tone look can be done with different colors, as shown below. You'll still achieve a sophisticated feeling!

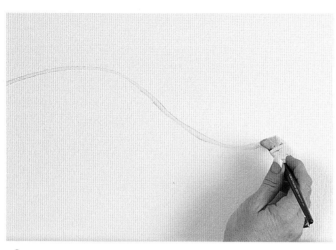

1 **PAINT THE VINE** To paint the vine, double load the ¾-inch (19mm) flat with Wicker White, Taupe, and floating medium. Use the chisel edge and lead with Wicker White.

2 Add extra vines off the main vine.

This pattern may be hand-traced or photocopied for personal use only. Enlarge at 200% to bring up to full size.

Walls should be cleaned or newly painted with eggshell or satin latex paint. Trace and transfer the pattern, or hang the pattern below the area to be painted and use for reference.

3 PAINT HEART-SHAPED LEAVES Using the same brush double loaded with Wicker White, Taupe and floating medium, place heart-shaped leaves at random with Wicker White on the outside edge.

4 ADD ONE-STROKE LEAVES Using the same brush and colors, paint one-stroke leaves at random.

5 ADD FIVE-PETAL HYDRANGEA Double load the no. 12 flat with Wicker White and Taupe; paint the clusters of five-petal hydrangea. Occasionally flip the brush, putting the Taupe to the outside edge to add variety and interest.

6 ADD ONE-STROKE & SHADOWY LEAVES Paint some small one-stroke leaves with the no. 12 flat. Paint some in all Taupe and some in all Wicker White. Work a lot of floating medium into the brush to paint some shadowy leaves. Add some curlicues throughout the design to mimic new growth.

dreamy lettering

We built this bed from scratch and left space at the top for painting. We decided to write a message to our grandchild rather than using other types of artwork. This type of border would look just as good on a wall instead of the top edge of a headboard.

I like to use messages in children's rooms that inspire and are uplifting. So leave a thoughtful message to your children or grandchildren!

PAINT: (A)=FOLKART ACRYLICS

Denim Blue
(A)

Midnight
(A)

SURFACE
• wooden headboard

BRUSHES
• no. 4 flat lettering
• no. 5 script lettering liner

ADDITIONAL SUPPLIES
• water

PAINT COLORS FOR COORDINATING BORDER

Basil Green
(A)

Thicket
(A)

Photos of the no. 4 flat lettering brush and the no. 5 script lettering liner are not available at this time

A COORDINATING BORDER Use inspirational words and phrases throughout the room. You can paint these on furniture, pillows or even up along the ceiling line.

1 **PAINT THE INSIDE LETTERS** Thin the Denim Blue paint with a little water. Use a no. 4 flat lettering brush to fill in the inside of the letters, using downward strokes.

2 **OUTLINING THE LETTERS** Use thinned Midnight and a no. 5 script lettering liner to outline. Push down to make thicker outlining and lift up to the tip for fine lines.

This pattern may be hand-traced or photocopied for personal use only. Enlarge at 200%, then enlarge again 125% to bring up to full size.

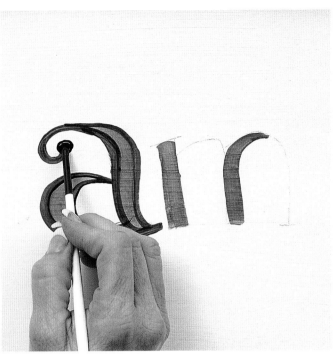

3 Pick up paint on the handle of the brush and dot where appropriate.

whimsical daisy

The inspiration for Brooke's room came from the design of loose vines and flowers on the sheer curtains. The wall color is very similar to a FolkArt paint color, Buttercrunch. I loved giving the room a three-dimensional effect by using flowers painted on vinyl flooring, cut out, and then attached to the vine with pop dots. Make sure your eyes catch all the surprises in this room.

PAINT: (A)=FOLKART ACRYLICS; (AP)=FOLKART ARTISTS' PIGMENTS; (M)=FOLKART METALLICS

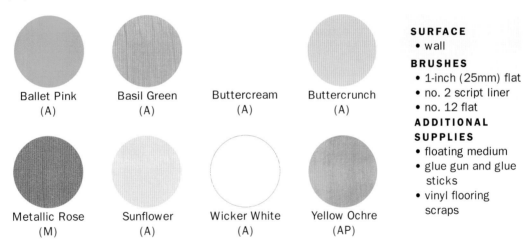

Ballet Pink (A)

Basil Green (A)

Buttercream (A)

Buttercrunch (A)

Metallic Rose (M)

Sunflower (A)

Wicker White (A)

Yellow Ochre (AP)

SURFACE
- wall

BRUSHES
- 1-inch (25mm) flat
- no. 2 script liner
- no. 12 flat

ADDITIONAL SUPPLIES
- floating medium
- glue gun and glue sticks
- vinyl flooring scraps

PAINT COLORS FOR COORDINATING BORDER

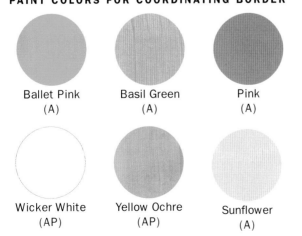

Ballet Pink (A)

Basil Green (A)

Pink (A)

Wicker White (AP)

Yellow Ochre (AP)

Sunflower (A)

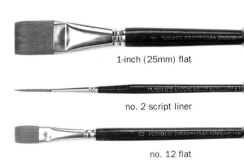

1-inch (25mm) flat

no. 2 script liner

no. 12 flat

This pattern may be hand-traced or photocopied for personal use only. Enlarge at 148% to bring up to full size.

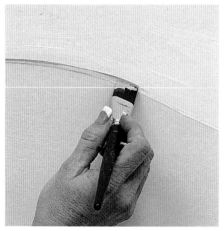

1 **PAINT THE VINE** Paint the wall and ceiling, bringing the ceiling color partly down the wall. Load a 1-inch (25mm) flat with Basil Green and floating medium. Using the chisel edge, paint a wavy green vine between the white and yellow wall color.

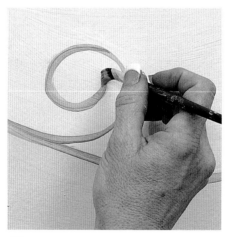

2 **PAINT THE CURLS** Load a no. 12 flat with Basil Green and floating medium. Use the chisel to paint curls.

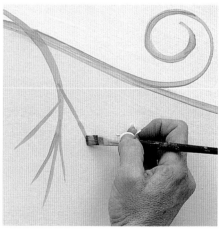

3 **ADD STEMS AND TENDRILS** Add a few additional tendrils, crossing over the main vine.

These patterns may be hand-traced or photocopied for personal use only. Enlarge at 138% to bring up to full size.

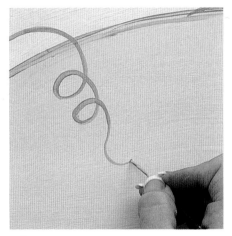

4 **PAINT SOME CURLICUES**
Load the no. 2 script liner with inky Basil Green; paint some curlicues.

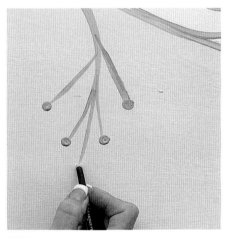

5 **ADD DOTS** With the handle of the no. 2 script liner and Basil Green, add dots onto the end of each stem.

TO PAINT THE FLOWERS:
Colors: Metallic Rose petals, details are Ballet Pink, center is Buttercream with Yellow Ochre details

Ballet Pink petals, details are Metallic Rose, center is Sunflower with Yellow Ochre details

TO PAINT THE STARS:
Colors: Sunflower, details are Wicker White, center is Ballet Pink with Metallic Rose details

TO PAINT THE BUTTERFLY:
Colors: Wings are Buttercream with Yellow Ochre details; body is Sunflower with Metallic Rose details

A COORDINATING BORDER
This is a smaller and slightly more detailed version of the border found on pages 74 and 78-79. It's the perfect size to paint on accessories such as a toy chest, lamp and even a doll's bed!

6 **TRACE AND PAINT THE VINYL FLOWERS, STARS, AND BUTTER-FLIES** Basecoat the back of vinyl flooring with Wicker White. Trace the flowers, stars, and butterflies on the vinyl. Use a no. 12 flat to basecoat (See colors on page 77.) Use two coats to get good coverage as you paint some of the details in each item.

7 Follow the same procedures for the other flowers using different color combinations.

8 **"STITCH" AROUND THE EDGES** Use a no. 2 script liner to paint broken lines for the "stitching."

9 Cut out shapes out of the vinyl.

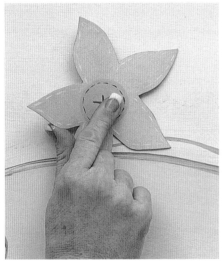

10 Glue onto the wall.

You can also place the flowers, stars, and butterflies on furniture, as shown on this armoire.

crowning glory

Elegant, simple, and easy. I like that combination. I started looking through clip art

books and also photos of iron railing that I had taken while in Europe. I enlarged and

then traced my chosen scroll ironwork right on the wall. Filling in the painting was the

easiest part of this job. Think how great this scrollwork would be with authentic coloring

to resemble real iron. The colors chosen here match the bedding in the master bedroom.

PAINT: (A)=FOLKART ACRYLICS; (AP)=FOLKART ARTISTS' PIGMENTS

Hauser Medium Green (AP)   Wicker White (A)   Yellow Light (AP)

SURFACE
• wall
BRUSHES
• no. 12 flat
ADDITIONAL SUPPLIES
• floating medium

PAINT COLORS FOR COORDINATING BORDER

Butter Pecan (A)   Wicker White (A)

no. 12 flat

This pattern may be hand-traced or photocopied for personal use only. Enlarge at
200%, then enlarge again at 200% to
bring up to full size.

This pattern may be hand-traced or photocopied for personal use only. Enlarge at
200%, then enlarge again at 200% to
bring up to full size. This is a simple
scroll. Similar patterns can be found on
the internet.

A COORDINATING BORDER This scrollwork border can
be used with the medallion shown on pg. 80. It can be painted vertically (see wall inset on pg. 80) or horizontally. One
idea: paint it above the baseboards in your room.

1 **LOADING THE BRUSH, FIRST STROKES** Load a no. 12 flat with Hauser Medium Green and occasional Wicker White, Yellow Light, or floating medium. Use the chisel edge and pull downward strokes.

2 Add some small, trailing scrolls off of the main scroll.

3 **COMMA STROKES** Add comma strokes to connect to the scroll.

4 **ADDITIONAL SCROLLWORK** Paint more scrollwork over the top of other scrolls to give it some dimension.

palm fronds

This bathroom had cabinets that needed some loving care and wallpaper that didn't go with the adjoining family room. I was afraid that this detail would be noticed by our guests when they visited with us.

I chose to use neutrals and some light metallic colors. Depending on your décor, you can use bright beach-like colors in blues and seafoam greens. These colors will create a tropical look.

PAINT: (A)=FOLKART ACRYLIC; (AP)=FOLKART ARTISTS' PIGMENTS; (M)=FOLKART METALLICS

Burnt Sienna
(AP)

Green Umber
(AP)

Inca Gold
(M)

LIcorice
(A)

SURFACE
• wall

BRUSHES
• 1-inch (25mm) flat
• 1¹⁄₂-inch (38mm) flat

ADDITIONAL SUPPLIES
• floating medium

PAINT COLORS FOR COORDINATING BORDER

Basil Green
(A)

Thicket
(A)

This is the same border used on pgs. 84 and 86–87. The colors have been changed, to appeal to those who like a more "natural" tropical look.

1-inch (25mm) flat

1¹⁄₂ inch (38mm) flat

This border is painted on a wall with a taupe/khaki Venetian plaster finish. You can paint the border over a flat, solid-color wall, wallpaper with a stripe or a faux-finish.

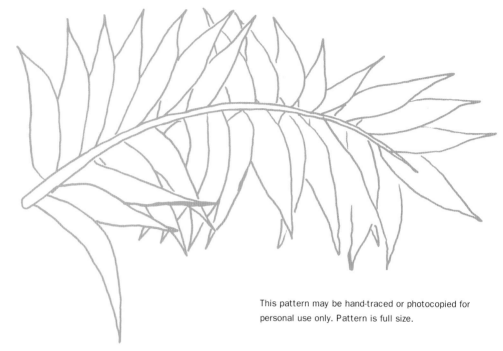

This pattern may be hand-traced or photocopied for personal use only. Pattern is full size.

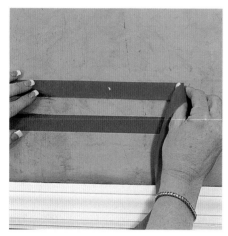

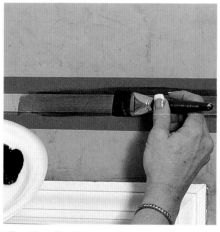

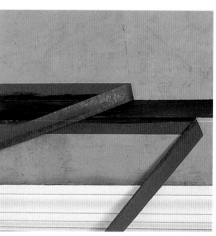

1 **PAINT THE BORDER** Tape the wall for the stripe at the top of the border. Measure from the ceiling to the top edge of the border. Place the bottom edge of the tape there. Measure around the room and place your tape.

2 Use floating medium and Licorice to paint the border. Make sure the border is NOT a solid color; keep it sheer.

3 Pull the tape before the paint dries.

4 **PAINT THE STEM** Using the 1-inch (25mm) flat, double load Green Umber and Burnt Sienna and paint the stem on the chisel. The stem is for placement.

5 **PAINT THE PALM FRONDS** Keep dipping in floating medium, Green Umber, and Burnt Sienna while you paint the fronds. The floating medium keeps the fronds somewhat transparent. Add a little Inca Gold to the leaf on occasion, especially over the black line, to add a little shimmer. Use the Inca Gold according to your taste.

6 Come back and clean up the stem with the same brush and colors.

7 Paint your frond stems at different angles for variety.

grapevines

Instead of curtains, I wanted to dress the laundry room with wild herbs, a twisted grapevine and insects buzzing around the blossoms. When you walk from the garage into this laundry room and look up, you see a garden. It makes me smile and say, "I did it myself."

PAINT: (A)=FOLKART ACRYLICS; (AP)=FOLKART ARTISTS' PIGMENTS

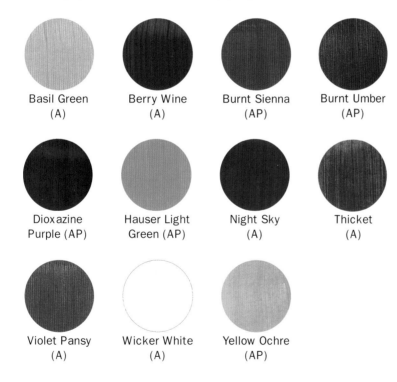

Basil Green
(A)

Berry Wine
(A)

Burnt Sienna
(AP)

Burnt Umber
(AP)

Dioxazine
Purple (AP)

Hauser Light
Green (AP)

Night Sky
(A)

Thicket
(A)

Violet Pansy
(A)

Wicker White
(A)

Yellow Ochre
(AP)

SAME COLORS ARE USED FOR COORDINATING BORDER

SURFACE
- wall

BRUSHES
- ¾-inch (19mm) flat
- 1-inch (25mm) flat
- no. 6 flat
- no. 12 flat
- no. 16 flat
- no. 10 filbert
- no. 2 script liner

ADDITIONAL SUPPLIES
- floating medium

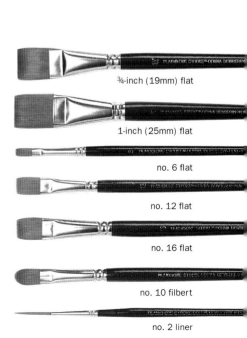

¾-inch (19mm) flat

1-inch (25mm) flat

no. 6 flat

no. 12 flat

no. 16 flat

no. 10 filbert

no. 2 liner

1 **PAINT A WINDING VINE** Double load a 1-inch (25mm) flat with Burnt Umber, Burnt Sienna and a little Wicker White. Paint a winding vine along the wall for placement.

This pattern may be hand-traced or photocopied for personal use only. Enlarge at 200%, then enlarge again by 152% to bring up to full size.

2 Add additional vines to fill in.

3 **PAINTING LEAVES** Using the same brush, add Thicket to the Burnt Umber side and Basil Green to the Burnt Sienna side. Add a touch of floating medium and paint the long skinny leaves. Paint clusters of these leaves throughout the vine.

4 Work the same dirty brush into a puddle of floating medium. Use this dirty puddle of paint to paint the soft shadow leaves.

5 **PAINT ONE-STROKE LEAVES** Use a no. 12 flat with Burnt Sienna and floating medium to paint one-stroke leaves.

6 **PAINT FLOWER CLUSTERS** Double load a no. 10 filbert with Violet Pansy and Wicker White; paint clusters of flowers. Touch and pull, touch and pull, leading with the Wicker White and pull back towards the vine.

7 These are the finished clusters.

8 **PAINT PETAL FLOWERS** Double load a no. 16 flat with Wicker White and Yellow Ochre. Keeping the Wicker White to the outer edge, paint a teardrop shape with a slight ruffled edge. Paint five to six of these petals to form the flower.

9 Use the chisel edge to paint the trailing flowers.

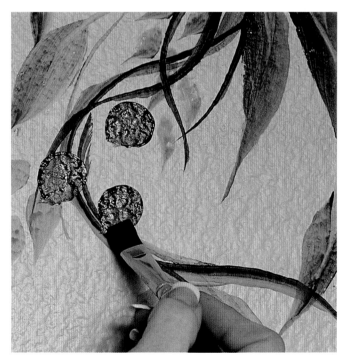

10 Dip the no. 2 script liner into Thicket and Hauser Light Green and dab on the center of the flowers.

11 **PAINT THE PODS** Double load the no. 16 flat with Berry Wine and Dioxazine Purple. Using the flat side of the brush with the Dioxazine Purple to the outer edge, paint the seed pods.

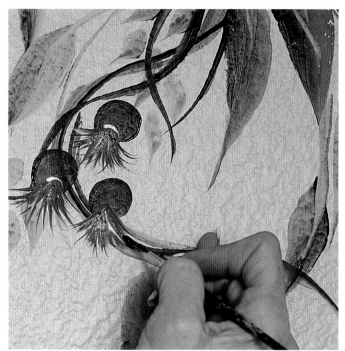

12 **PAINT THE PODS (CONT.)** Double load a no. 12 flat with Dioxazine Purple and Wicker White. Using the chisel edge and leading with the Wicker White, paint the stems of the pod. If it is too dark or too light, flip the brush and paint additional stems.

13 Load Dioxazine Purple on the no. 2 script liner and add finer detail. Stroke your brush through Wicker White and paint the accent where all the strokes come out.

14 **PAINT THE SWEET PEAS** Double load the no. 16 flat with Wicker White and Night Sky, with the Wicker White to the outer edge. Paint wiggle strokes to form sweet peas.

15 Paint the first layer, then come back and paint additional layers.

16 Double load the no. 12 flat with Burnt Umber and Hauser Light Green to paint the stem and attach to the vine. Pull on the chisel from the base of the flower to one point. Then pull them all to the stem.

17 **PAINT THE FERN FRONDS** Dab on fern fronds, using the ¾-inch (19mm) flat with Wicker White.

Make sure to paint large open grapevines. You'll love the winding vines so much you might decide not to paint the flowering herbs. I used colors from the other rooms in the house that can be seen from this laundry room. This helps to pull the décor together.

18 **PAINT THE BEE** To paint the bee, use a no. 12 flat with Yellow Ochre and paint a one-stroke leaf for the body.

19 Use a no. 2 script liner with Burnt Umber to paint the head and details on the body. Use the tip of the brush to paint short little strokes.

20 With the same brush, paint antennas and trailing lines.

21 Use a no. 10 filbert with Wicker White to paint the wings (push, pull, push, pull).

22 **PAINT THE DRAGONFLY**
To paint the dragonfly, use a no. 2 script liner with Burnt Umber to paint the antennas. Use a no. 6 flat with Burnt Umber to paint small segments to create the body, painting smaller segments towards the bottom.

23 With the no. 12 flat and a lot of floating medium and a little Wicker White, paint wings. Let dry thoroughly.

24 Use a no. 2 script liner and inky Burnt Umber to paint the details on the wings. With the tip of the brush, outline the wing and then add small details inside the wings.

25 **FINISHING DETAILS**
Paint curlicues with the no. 2 script liner and inky Burnt Umber.

COORDINATING BORDER The border on the bottom of the page is a "toned down" variation of the border shown above it and also shown on pg. 88. This shows that neutrals and subtle colors also can add a lot of impact and pattern to any surface.

clothesline

I think a laundry room should have a fun and bright look. Raising seven children created a lot of laundry for me to wash! I did not like to look at dull, drab walls every day, so I made the walls fun and entertaining.

I loved painting a clothesline and filling it with painted clothing. Use your own clothing and accessories as "patterns." Adapt your painting to what reminds you of your family. With all the new grandbabies we have, I just had to paint a diaper!

On the next page, check out the real aprons used as curtains that we added for a three-dimensional effect and to complete the room.

PAINT: (A)=FOLKART ACRYLICS; (AP)=FOLKART ARTISTS' PIGMENTS

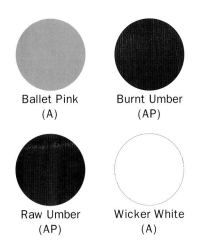

Ballet Pink
(A)

Burnt Umber
(AP)

Raw Umber
(AP)

Wicker White
(A)

SURFACE
• wall

BRUSHES
• ³/₄-inch (19mm) flat
• 1-inch (25mm) flat
• no. 12 flat
• no. 2 script liner

ADDITIONAL SUPPLIES
• sponge painter
• floating medium
• glue gun and glue sticks
• wooden or plastic clothes pins

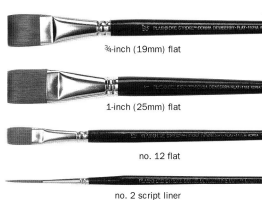

¾-inch (19mm) flat

1-inch (25mm) flat

no. 12 flat

no. 2 script liner

Pencil where the clothesline is going to be. Pencil in the shapes of each piece of clothing (you can even use your own clothing as a pattern). Paint the clothes on the clothesline in colors that coordinate with your décor.

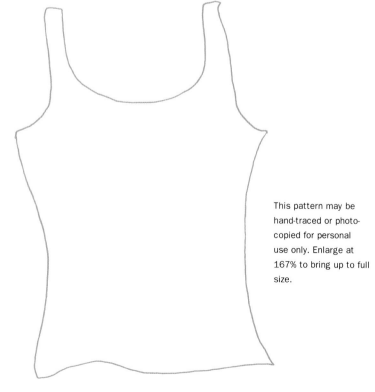

This pattern may be hand-traced or photocopied for personal use only. Enlarge at 167% to bring up to full size.

HOW TO PAINT THE CAMISOLE

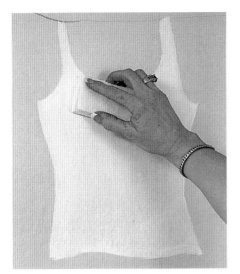

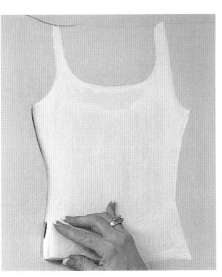

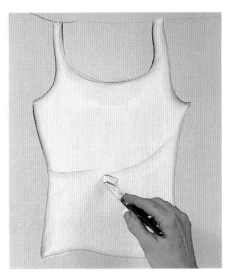

1 BASECOAT THE CAMISOLE Basecoat the camisole using a sponge painter and Wicker White. Keep the camisole somewhat sheer.

2 OUTLINE THE CAMISOLE Go over the camisole edge with the sponge painter with Wicker White and a side load of Raw Umber.

3 ADD "WRINKLES" Use your 1-inch (25mm) brush with a side load of Raw Umber and floating medium, to clean up edges and add "wrinkles."

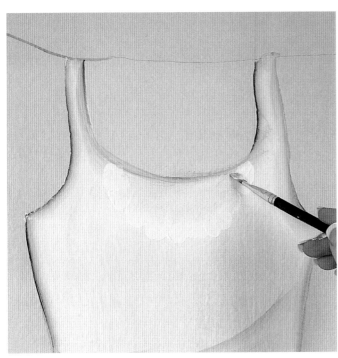

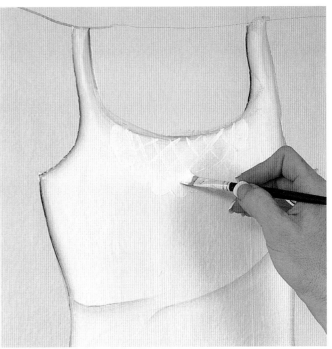

4 ADD A RUFFLE Use a no. 12 flat and Wicker White to paint a ruffle onto the camisole.

5 With the chisel edge, add some detail to the lacy area.

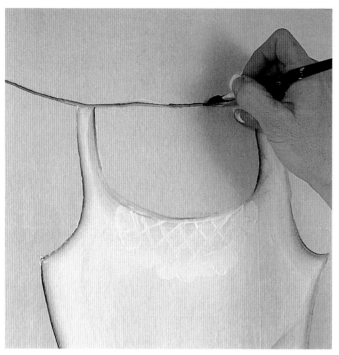

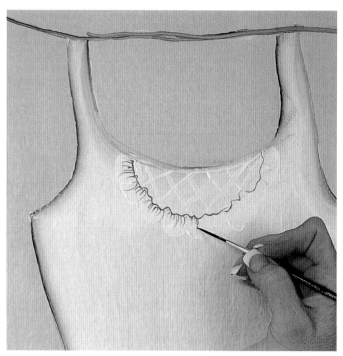

6 **PAINT THE CLOTHESLINE** Double load a ¾-inch (19mm) flat with Burnt Umber and Wicker White and paint the clothesline.

7 **ADD ACCENTS** Add accents to the camisole with a no. 2 script liner and inky Raw Umber.

PAINT CLOTHING & ACCESSORIES ALL ALONG THE CLOTHESLINE TO CREATE THE BORDER

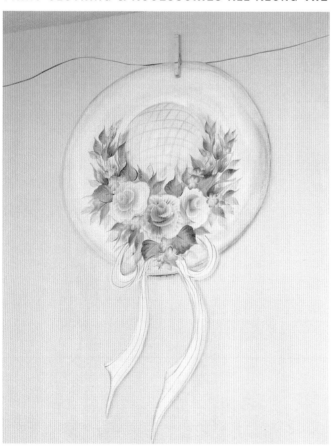

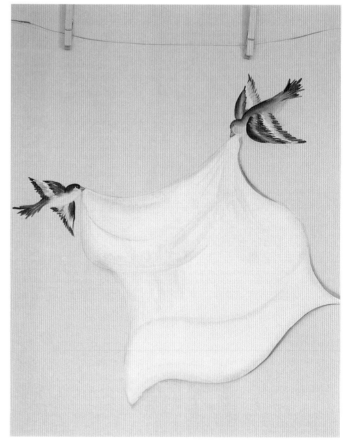

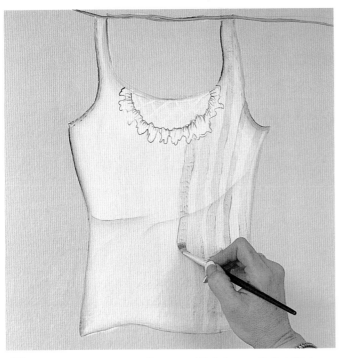

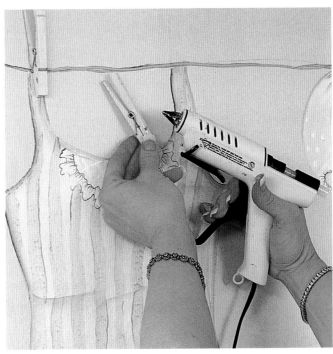

8 **PAINT STRIPES** On a no. 12 flat, use Ballet Pink and floating medium to paint the stripes.

9 **ADD CLOTHESPINS** To add a realistic detail, use your glue gun to glue on wooden clothespins.

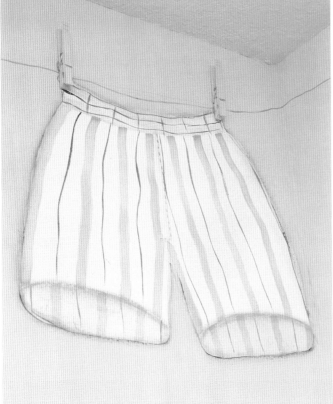

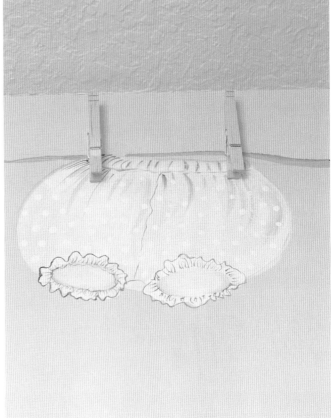

animal parade

The wide stripes of fresh, soft-tone colors below the chair rail is where my decorating idea started. The stripes reminded me of the sections of a fence. I then decided that the children would really enjoy animals peeping over the top of the "fence." Rather than painting the animals in their natural colors, I made them fun and bright. To do this I limited my colors, keeping them comical and slightly cartoonish. Think outside the box when choosing colors. Use children's coloring books for inspiration; simplify the line drawings to create your own collection.

PAINT: (A)=FOLKART ACRYLICS; (AP)=FOLKART ARTISTS' PIGMENTS

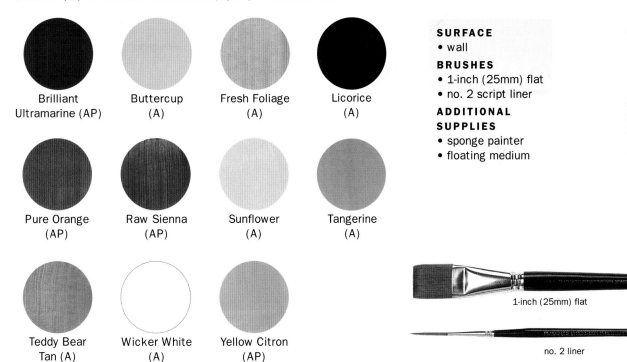

Brilliant Ultramarine (AP)

Buttercup (A)

Fresh Foliage (A)

Licorice (A)

Pure Orange (AP)

Raw Sienna (AP)

Sunflower (A)

Tangerine (A)

Teddy Bear Tan (A)

Wicker White (A)

Yellow Citron (AP)

SURFACE
• wall

BRUSHES
• 1-inch (25mm) flat
• no. 2 script liner

ADDITIONAL SUPPLIES
• sponge painter
• floating medium

1-inch (25mm) flat

no. 2 liner

This pattern may be hand-traced or photocopied for personal use only. Enlarge at 200%, then enlarge again at 152% to bring up to full size.

1 **BASE IN THE ELEPHANT SHAPE** Double load the round side of the moistened sponge painter with Brilliant Ultramarine and Wicker White. Keeping the Brilliant Ultramarine to the outer edge, base in the shape.

2 Add the ears, and then the head and trunk.

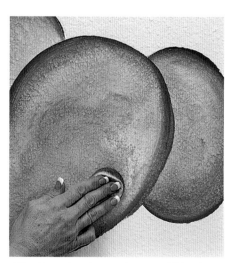

3 Use circular motions to fill in the center area. This has more of a "watercolor" look than a heavy opaque finish. Make sure you use two colors, one light and one dark, to create that soft look.

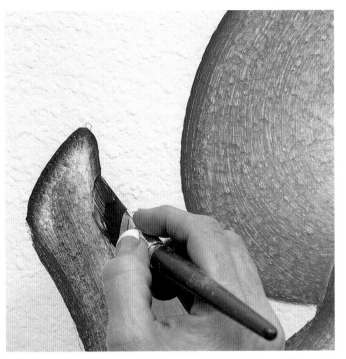

4 **ADD DETAIL & DEFINITION** Load a 1-inch (25mm) flat with floating medium and then side load a touch of Brilliant Ultramarine. Stroke along the edges that need more detail and definition.

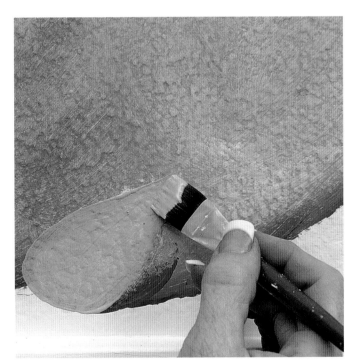

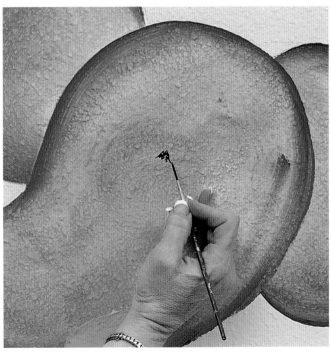

5 **PAINT THE MOUTH** Load the 1-inch (25mm) flat with Tangerine and paint the mouth.

6 **PAINT THE EYES** Load the no. 2 script liner with inky Licorice; paint the eyes.

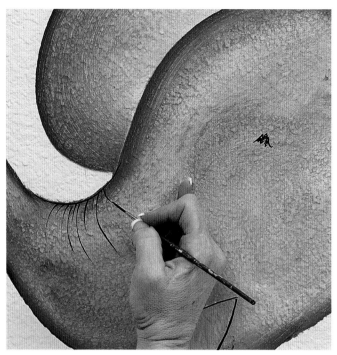

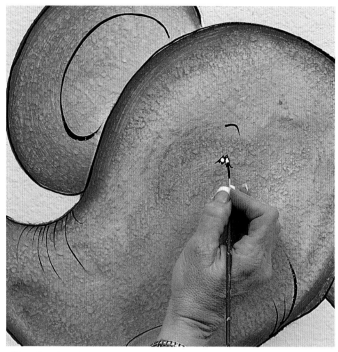

7 **ADD OTHER DETAILS** Add additional details using the same brush. The wrinkles and folds are painted with short, little, curving strokes.

8 Stroke the same brush through the Wicker White; add one big dot in the eye. Add small dots to highlight.

FINISHED ELEPHANT

PAINTING THE OTHER ANIMALS

CAMEL: Body is Teddy Bear Tan, touch of Raw Sienna; eye highlights are Wicker White; details are inky Licorice

LAMB: Face is Tangerine and a touch of Wicker White; legs are Wicker White and enough Licorice to create a gray tone; fur is Wicker White; details are inky Licorice

COW: Body is Wicker White; one side of face and body spots are Wicker White with a touch of Licorice to create a gray tone; hooves and flower are Buttercup and Sunflower; details are inky Licorice

All patterns may be hand-traced or photocopied for personal use only. Enlarge at 200%, then enlarge at 200% again to bring up to full size.

BEAR: Body is Brilliant Ultramarine and a touch of Wicker White; snout is Buttercup; nose is Raw Sienna; outline and details are inky Licorice

BROWN DOG: Body and nose are Teddy Bear Tan; eyes are Wicker White; details are inky Licorice

HORSE: Body is Wicker White and enough Licorice to create a gray tone; teeth are Wicker White; tongue is Tangerine; hat is Brilliant Ultramarine and Wicker White; details are inky Licorice

PIGLET: Body is Tangerine and a touch of Buttercup; eye highlights are Wicker White; details are inky Licorice

All patterns may be hand-traced or photocopied for personal use only. Enlarge at 200%, then enlarge at 200& again to bring up to full size.

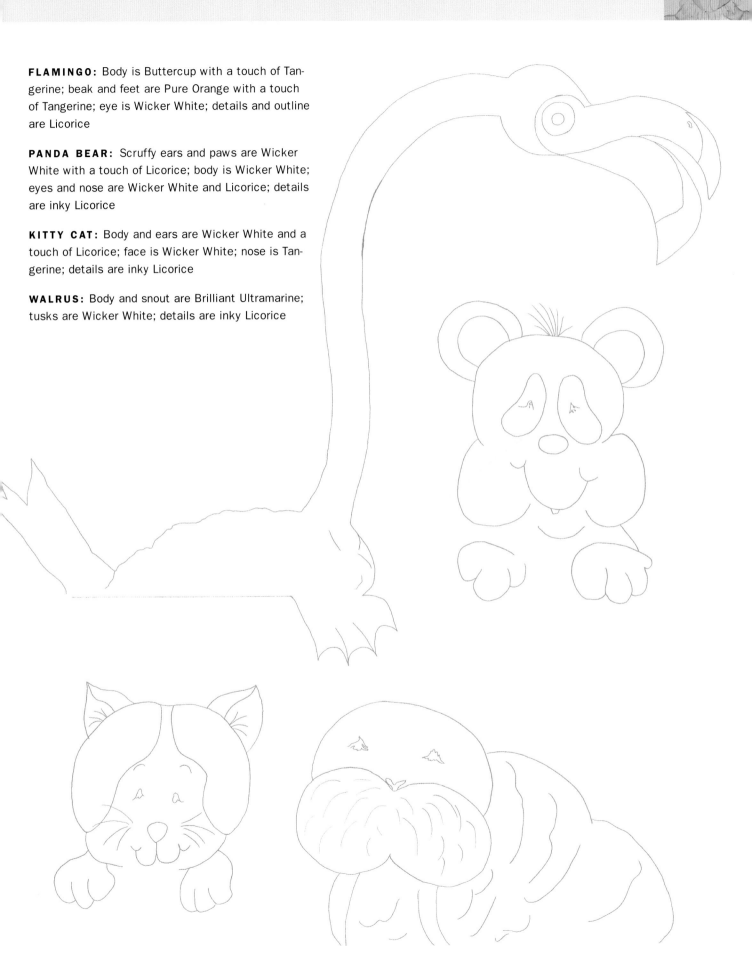

FLAMINGO: Body is Buttercup with a touch of Tangerine; beak and feet are Pure Orange with a touch of Tangerine; eye is Wicker White; details and outline are Licorice

PANDA BEAR: Scruffy ears and paws are Wicker White with a touch of Licorice; body is Wicker White; eyes and nose are Wicker White and Licorice; details are inky Licorice

KITTY CAT: Body and ears are Wicker White and a touch of Licorice; face is Wicker White; nose is Tangerine; details are inky Licorice

WALRUS: Body and snout are Brilliant Ultramarine; tusks are Wicker White; details are inky Licorice

MOTHER OSTRICH: Body is Yellow Citron; beak is Tangerine; cheek is Wicker White; details are inky Licorice

BABY OSTRICHES: Body is Buttercup and a side load of Sunflower; details are inky Licorice

LION: Body is Teddy Bear Tan and a touch of Raw Sienna; mane and snout are Buttercup; nose is Raw Sienna; details are inky Licorice

BEAVER: Body is Buttercup with a touch of Sunflower; teeth are Wicker White; details and outline are inky Licorice

All patterns may be hand-traced or photocopied for personal use only. Enlarge at 200&, then enlarge at 200% again to bring up to full size.

GIRAFFE: Body is Buttercup and Sunflower; spots and neck hair are Tangerine and Sunflower with an occasional touch of Pure Orange; horns are Fresh Foliage; flower is Pure Orange, Tangerine, and a touch of Buttercup; nose is Wicker White and a touch of Licorice; details are inky Licorice

MONKEY: Body is Tangerine and a touch of Pure Orange; eyes are Wicker White; details are inky Licorice

POODLE: Body is Wicker White and a touch of Licorice; nose and collar are Buttercup and Teddy Bear Tan; details are inky Licorice

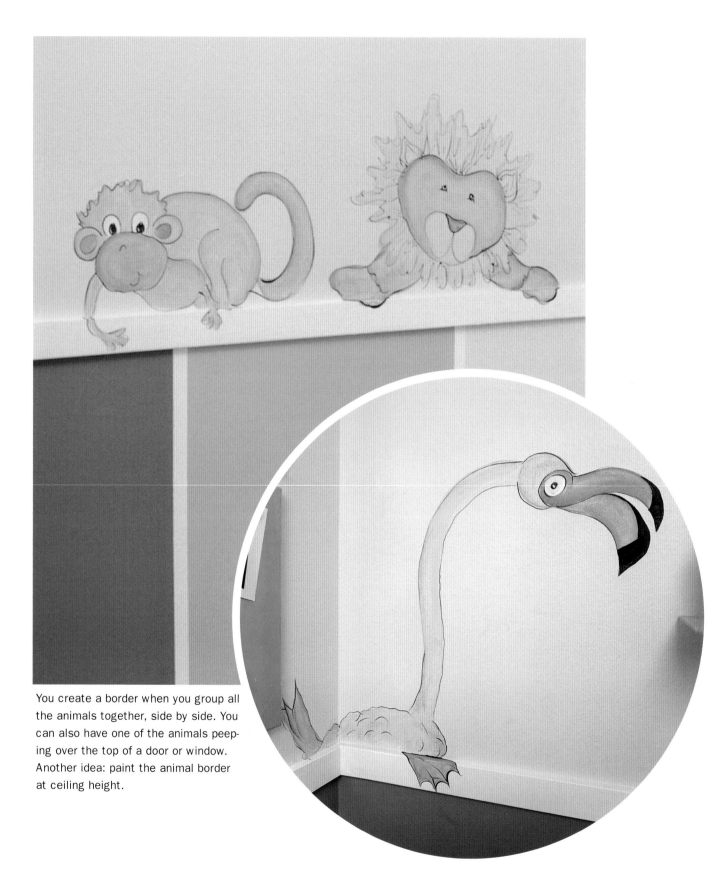

You create a border when you group all the animals together, side by side. You can also have one of the animals peeping over the top of a door or window. Another idea: paint the animal border at ceiling height.

If you don't have room to paint all the animals, pick and choose your favorites. What about a border of farm animals!

magic beanstalk

This little attic serves as a secret hideaway for my special grandbabies. I wanted the place to be all theirs—a place where they could dream of climbing to the sky and imagine all kinds of adventures. But most of all, I wanted a place where they could have fun! I'm sure they will always know that this was painted and created just for them and came from their Mima's heart.

PAINT: (A)=FOLKART ACRYLICS; (AP)=FOLKART ARTISTS' PIGMENTS

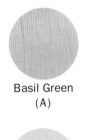

Basil Green (A)

Brilliant Ultramarine (AP)

Fresh Foliage (A)

Grass Green (A)

Medium Yellow (AP)

Thicket (A)

Violet Pansy (A)

Wicker White (A)

SURFACE
- wall

BRUSHES
- ¾-inch (19mm) flat
- 1-inch (25mm) flat
- 1½-inch (38mm) flat
- 2-inch (51mm) flat
- no. 12 flat
- no. 2 script liner
- scruffy

ADDITIONAL SUPPLIES
- sponge painter
- floating medium

PAINT COLORS FOR COORDINATING BORDER

Brilliant Ultramarine (AP)

Fresh Foliage (A)

Licorice (A)

School Bus Yellow (A)

Thicket (A)

Violet Pansy (A)

Wicker White (A)

Yellow Light (AP)

¾-inch (19mm) flat

1-inch (25mm) flat

1½-inch (38mm) flat

2-inch (51mm) flat

no. 12 flat

no. 2 script liner

scruffy

These patterns may be hand-traced or photocopied for personal use only. Enlarge at 200% to bring up to full size.

1 **PAINT THE BEANSTALK** Multi-load the sponge painter with Basil Green and Thicket. Pick up a little Grass Green and Fresh Foliage as you go. Base in the beanstalk. Keep the darkest color to the bottom edge. Add floating medium as needed to help spread the paint.

2 Double load the 1-inch (25mm) flat with Thicket and floating medium. Shade under the twists in the vine.

3 Double load the no. 12 flat with Thicket and Basil Green; use the chisel edge to add accent curls.

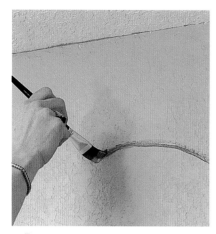

4 PAINT LARGE LEAVES
Double load the 1-inch (25mm) flat with Basil Green and Thicket. Using the flat side of the brush, paint the large leaves. Pick up some Grass Green and Fresh Foliage occasionally to add variation.

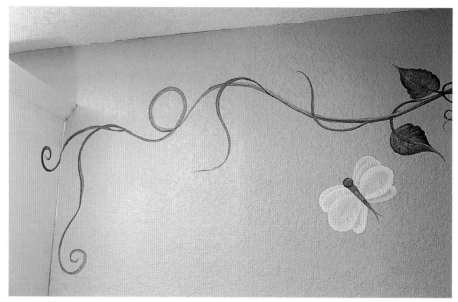

5 Add extra vines and curls at the end.

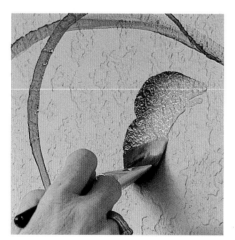

6 PAINT THE LARGE BEAN LEAVES Use Basil Green, Thicket and a small amount of Grass Green to paint the multi-stroke bean leaves at the end of the curling vines. Double load the 2-inch (51mm) flat with Basil Green and Thicket; add a touch of Grass Green for variation. Use the flat side of the brush with Thicket to the outer edge; paint the three curved strokes to form the leaf.

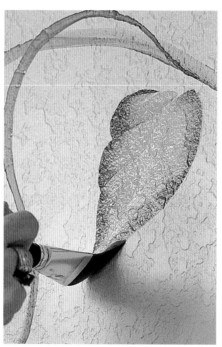

7 Using the same brush and colors, paint the other side by making one long, smooth, sliding stroke.

8 Use the chisel edge to pull a stem into the middle.

9 **PAINT THE DRAGONFLY** Double load the ¾-inch (19mm) flat with Fresh Foliage and Thicket; paint the body of the dragonfly using teardrop strokes to make the sections. (Pattern on page 118.)

10 Load a 1-inch (25mm) flat with floating medium and then side load with Wicker White. Using the flat side of the brush and keeping the Wicker White to the outer edge, paint the wings. Use the Wicker White edge of the brush to shape the wing.

11 Double load the 1-inch (25mm) flat with Fresh Foliage and Thicket; paint the head.

12 Double load the scruffy with Medium Yellow and Wicker White; pounce the cheeks. Dip the handle of the no. 2 script liner into Fresh Foliage and make two dots for the ends of the antennas. Then load the no. 2 script liner with Thicket and pull the antennas to connect. Dot the nose with Thicket using the handle of the brush. Use the no. 2 script liner and inky Thicket to paint the mouth.

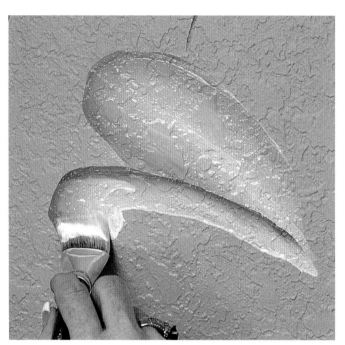

13 **PAINT ANOTHER DRAGONFLY** Load the 1½-inch (38mm) flat with Wicker White and then side load with Brilliant Ultramarine. Add some floating medium to create a slightly transparent color.

14 Keeping the Brilliant Ultramarine to the outer edge, paint the wings for the dragonfly.

15 Double load the 1-inch (25mm) flat with Fresh Foliage and Thicket and paint one-stroke leaf strokes to make the body segments.

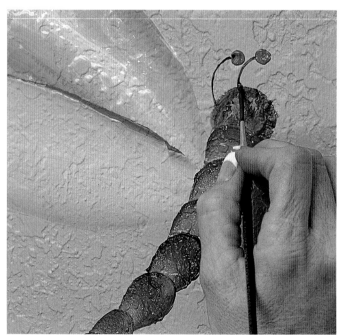

16 **PAINT THE HEAD & FACE** Dip the handle of the no. 12 into Fresh Foliage and make two large dots for the ends of the antennas. Then load the no. 2 script liner with Thicket and pull the antennas to connect.

17 Dot the nose with Thicket using the handle of the brush. Load the Scruffy with Medium Yellow and Wicker White; pounce the cheeks.

18 Use the no. 2 script liner and inky Medium Yellow to paint the mouth.

19 **PAINT THE BUTTERFLY** Double load the 1-inch (25mm) flat with Wicker White and Violet Pansy; paint the butterfly wings. Use the chisel edge to paint the bottom two wings.

20 Double load a 1-inch (25mm) flat with Fresh Foliage and Thicket. Paint a teardrop shape to form the head.

21 Double load the 1-inch (25mm) flat with Fresh Foliage and Thicket. Using the flat side of the brush and keeping the Fresh Foliage to the outside, paint the main body of the butterfly. Use the chisel edge to pull a line to end the body.

22 **PAINT THE FACE & ADD DETAILS** Load the scruffy with Medium Yellow; pounce on the cheeks. Dot antennas with Fresh Foliage using the handle of the brush and pull the antennas with the no. 2 script liner.

23 Dot the eyes and pull a line for the mouth using the no. 2 script liner and Thicket. Drag a script liner through thick Wicker White and add highlights in the eyes.

24 Double load the 1-inch (25mm) flat with Wicker White and Medium Yellow. Using the chisel edge of the brush and leading with the Wicker White, paint the comma strokes in the center of the wings. Use the handle of a brush to make the dots and a circle on the lower wings.

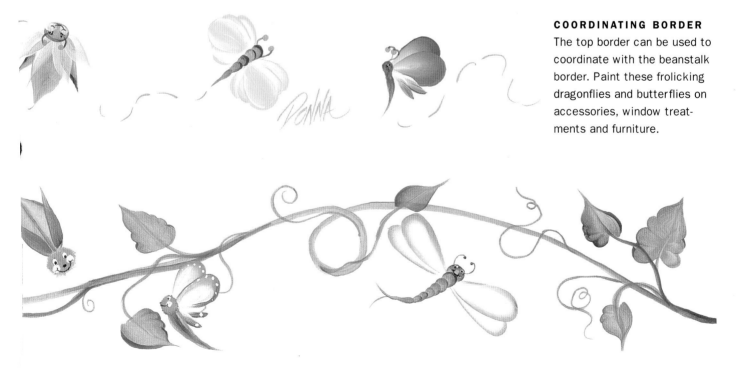

COORDINATING BORDER
The top border can be used to coordinate with the beanstalk border. Paint these frolicking dragonflies and butterflies on accessories, window treatments and furniture.

resources

PAINTS & BRUSHES:
PLAID ENTERPRISES, INC.
3225 Westech Drive
Norcross, GA 30092-3500
USA
Tel: 1-800-842-4197
www.plaidonline.com

DEWBERRY DESIGNS, INC.
365 Citrus Tower Blvd., Suite 106
Clermont, FL 32711
USA
Tel: 1-800-536-2627
www.onestroke.com

CANADIAN RETAILERS:
CRAFTS CANADA
Tel: 1-877-55CRAFT
www.craftscanada.ca

FOLK ART ENTERPRISES
P.O. Box 1088
Ridgetown, ON, N0P 2C0
Tel: 1-800-265-9434
www.folkartenterprises.com

MACPHERSON CRAFT
WHOLESALE
91 Queen St. E.
P.O. Box 1810
St. Mary's, ON, N4X 1C2
Tel: 1-800-238-6663
www.macphersoncrafts.com

MAUREEN MCNAUGHTON
ENTERPRISES, INC.
RR #2
Belwood, ON, N0B 1J0
Tel: 519-843-5648
Fax: 519-843-6022
www.maureen.mcnaughton.com

MERCURY ART & CRAFT
SUPERSHOP
16-332 Wellington St.
London, ON, N6C 4P6
Tel: 519-434-1637

TOWN & COUNTRY
FOLK ART SUPPLIES
93 Green Lane
Thornhill, ON, L3T 6K6
Tel: 905-882-0199

U.K. RETAILERS:
ART EXPRESS
Design House
Sizers Court
Yeadon LS19 7DP
Tel: 0800 731 4185
www.artexpress.co.uk

ATLANTIS EUROPEAN LTD.
7–9 Plumber's Row
London E1 1EQ
Tel: 020 7377 8855
www.atlantisart.co.uk

CRAFTS WORLD (HEAD OFFICE)
No. 8 North Street
Guildford
Surrey GU1 4 AF
Tel: 0700 757070

GREEN & STONE
259 King's Road
Chelsea
London SW3 5EL
Tel: 020 7352 6521

HOBBY CRAFTS (HEAD OFFICE)
River Court
Southern Sector
Bournemouth International Airport
Christchurch
Dorset BH23 6SE
Tel: 0800 272387

HOMECRAFTS DIRECT
P.O. Box 38
Leicester LE1 9BU
Tel: 0116 2697733
www.homecrafts.co.uk

index

Acrylic lacquers, 8
Angular brushes, 6
    loading, 12
    painting vines, 14
Animal Parade, 104-115
Antiqued effect, 41

Background, sponging color, 34
Basecoating, 76, 101
    with sponge painter, 106
Beak, 30
Beanstalk, 119
Bear, 110
Beaver, 112
Bee, 95-96
Berries, 26
Bird, 27-28, 30-31
Border, coordinating, 29, 42-43,
    53, 55, 65, 71, 77, 82, 97
Brush caddy, 6
Brushes, 6
    loading, 8-13, 83
Brushstrokes
    comma stroke, 20, 50, 56-
        57, 83
    C-stroke, 20, 63-64
    finishing, 52
    lettering, 49-50
    multi-stroke leaf, 17
    one-stroke leaves, 18, 40,
        45, 62, 69, 92
Butterfly, 77, 123-125

Camel, 109, 115
Camisole, 101
Cat, 111, 115
Chairs, painting coordinated ele-
    ments on, 42
Clothesline, 98-103
Clothespins, gluing on, 103
Comma stroke, 20, 50, 56, 83
Cow, 109
Crackling, 48
Crowning Glory, 80-83
C-stroke, 20, 63-64
Curlicues, 13, 27, 45, 65, 77
Curls, 76

Dog
    brown, 110, 115
    poodle, 113, 115

Dots, 77
Dragonfly, 96-97, 121-123
Dreamy Lettering, 70-73

Elephant, 106-108
Eyes
    bird, 30
    elephant, 107

Face, butterfly, 124
Fantasy Fruit, 32-45
Feathers, 28
Ferns, 61
    fronds, 95
    leaves, 37, 45
Filbert brush, loading, 13
Finish
    aged, 41, 57
    for table, 45
Flamingo, 111, 114
Flat brushes, 6
    painting vines, 14
Floating medium, 6
    adding, 10
Flower clusters, 92
Flowers, 77, 93
    five-petal, 19, 62-63
    hydrangea, 69
    sweet peas, 94
    trumpet, 63
FolkArt products, 6
Fonts, 73
Fruit
    grapes, 39-40
    pear, 37-39, 44
    plum, 38-39, 44

Giraffe, 113
Grape leaves, 36
Grapes, 39-40, 44
Grapevines, 88-97
Graphite paper, 49
Green Meadow, 58-65

Heart-shaped leaves, 15-16, 69
Horse, 110
Hydrangea, 69

Ivy leaves, 25

Lacquers, acrylic, 8

Lamb, 109
Leaves, 35, 61
    adding to scroll, 56-57
    clusters, 91
    fern, 37, 45, 95
    grape, 36
    heart-shaped, 15-16, 69
    ivy, 25
    large, 120
    multi-stroke, 17
    wiggle, 52
    See also Palm fronds
Leaves, one-stroke, 18, 69, 92
    filling in with, 40, 45, 62
Lettering, 49-50, 72-73
    transferring, 21
Liner brushes, 6, 12
Lion, 112, 114
Loading techniques, 8-13, 83

Magic Beanstalk, 116-125
Masking tape, 86-87
Medium. See Floating medium
Metallic paints, 6
Monkey, 113-114
Mouth, elephant, 107
Multi-loading, 10
Multi-stroke leaves, 17

One-stroke leaves, 18, 40, 45,
    62, 69, 92
Ostriches, 112
Outlining, 72, 101
    with broken lines, 78

Paint, 6
Palette, 6
Palm Fronds, 84-87
Palm fronds, 37, 87
Panda bear, 111
Pattern, transferring, 8
Pears, 37-39, 44
Penciling in, 100
Piglet, 110
Pigments, 6
Plum, 38-39, 44
Pods, 25, 51, 93-94
Pouncing, 11

Resources, 126
Ruffle, 101

Script liner. See Liner brushes
Scrollwork, 54-57, 83
Scruffy brushes, 6
    loading, 11
Shading, 27, 31, 50
Shapes
    basing in, 106
    penciling in, 100
    sponging, 21
    vinyl, 78-79
Shell, painting, 15
Sponge painter, 6-8
Sponging
    background color, 34
    basing in shape, 106
    shapes, 21
Stamens, 64-65
Stars, 77
Stems, 76, 87
Stripes, 103
Supplies, 6-8
Sweet peas, 94

Table border, 46-53
    coordinated, 42-45
Tail feathers, 28
Tone-on-Tone, 66-69
Tracing paper, 8
Transferring
    lettering, 21
    pattern, 8
Trumpet flower, 63

Vine(s), 24, 35, 60, 68, 76
    technique for painting, 14,
    24
    winding, 90-91, 95
Vine & Berries, 22-31
Vinyl shapes, three-dimensional,
    78-79

Wall preparation, 68, 86
Walrus, 111, 115
Whimsical Daisy, 74-79
Words to Live By, 46-53
Wrinkles, 101

The best in decorative painting instruction and inspiration is from NORTH LIGHT BOOKS!

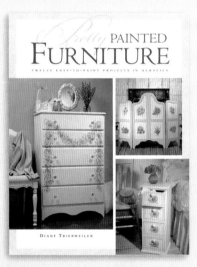

Add beauty and elegance to every room in your home! Diane Treirweiler shows you how with step-by-step instructions for giving old furniture a facelift and new furniture a personal touch. Twelve lovely projects, complete with helpful color charts and traceable patterns, teach you how to paint everything from berries to butterflies on chests, chairs, tables and more.

ISBN 1-58180-234-X, paperback, 128 pages, #32009-K

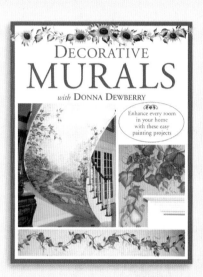

Renowned decorative painting instructor Donna Dewberry shares with you, step-by-step, some of her favorite tricks and techniques for creating trompe l'oeil murals, floral designs, faux finishes, popular theme designs and more. Donna's clear and encouraging instruction is filled with expert tips for doing each job a little faster and easier, along with answers to common questions about surface preparation, tools and paints!

ISBN 0-89134-988-X, paperback, 144 pages, #31459-K

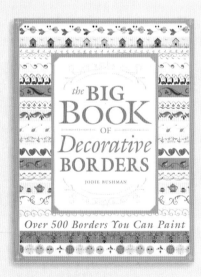

This one-of-a-kind book is a must-have reference! With this comprehensive guide, you'll learn to create an amazing variety of borders and embellishments using the simplest of strokes. You'll find over 500 border designs that you can fashion with different elements including flowers, leaves, vines, scrolls, shells, lace, ribbons, bows, children's themes and more! Also included are guidelines for measuring and marking walls and window frames to make your wall border painting easy!

ISBN 1-58180-335-4, paperback, 144 pages, #32303-K

Add drama to any room in your home with one of these eleven delightful mini-murals! They're perfect when you don't have the time or the experience to tackle a whole wall. You'll learn exactly which colors and brushes to use, plus tips and mini-demos on how to get that realistic "wow" effect mural painters love. Detailed templates, instructions and photos assure your success at every step.

ISBN 1-58180-145-9, paperback, 144 pages, #31891-K

These and other fine North Light titles are available from your local craft retailer, bookstore, online supplier, or by calling 1-800-448-0915.